Mastering SAP Business ByDesign: A Comprehensive Guide to Streamline Your Business

Chapter 1: Introduction to SAP Business ByDesign

Welcome to the world of SAP Business ByDesign! In this chapter, we will introduce you to the fundamentals of SAP Business ByDesign and provide you with a solid understanding of its capabilities, features, and benefits. Let's get started!

1.1 Understanding SAP Business ByDesign

SAP Business ByDesign is a cloud-based enterprise resource planning (ERP) solution designed to streamline and integrate various business processes. It offers a comprehensive suite of modules, including finance, sales, marketing, procurement, inventory management, project management, human resources, and more.

ByDesign is specifically tailored for small and medium-sized businesses (SMBs), providing them with a flexible and scalable solution to manage their operations efficiently. With its user-friendly interface and intuitive navigation, even non-technical users can easily leverage its power.

1.2 Key Features and Benefits

SAP Business ByDesign offers several key features and benefits that make it a popular choice among businesses:

a. Integrated Business Processes: ByDesign seamlessly integrates different aspects of your business, allowing data to flow across various modules in real-time. This integration enhances collaboration, reduces data redundancy, and enables better decision-making.

b. Scalability and Flexibility: Whether you have a small business or are experiencing rapid growth, ByDesign can scale to meet your evolving needs. It provides flexibility to add or modify modules, adjust user access, and adapt to changing business requirements.

c. Cloud-Based Deployment: ByDesign operates in the cloud, which means you can access it anytime, anywhere, as long as you have an internet connection. This eliminates the need for on-premises infrastructure, reduces IT costs, and ensures automatic updates and maintenance.

d. Mobile Access: ByDesign offers mobile applications that allow you to access critical business information on your smartphones or tablets. Stay connected with your business even while on the go and make informed decisions from anywhere.

e. Analytics and Reporting: ByDesign provides powerful reporting and analytics capabilities, allowing you to gain valuable insights into your business performance. With pre-built reports, customizable dashboards, and data visualization tools, you can monitor key metrics and make data-driven decisions.

1.3 Industry Applications

SAP Business ByDesign caters to a wide range of industries, including manufacturing, professional services, wholesale distribution, retail, and more. The solution offers industry-specific functionalities and best practices to address unique business requirements.

Whether you're in manufacturing and need to manage production orders, in professional services and require project-based billing, or in retail and need inventory management capabilities, ByDesign provides the necessary tools and functionalities to streamline your operations.

In the upcoming chapters, we will delve deeper into each module of SAP Business ByDesign, exploring their features and demonstrating how to effectively utilize them to optimize your business processes.

Congratulations! You have now completed the first chapter of our tutorial book, "Mastering SAP Business ByDesign." In the next chapter, we will guide you through the process of setting up your SAP Business ByDesign account and help you navigate the user interface.

Stay tuned for an exciting journey ahead, where you'll acquire the knowledge and skills to leverage the full potential of SAP Business ByDesign for your business success!

1.4 How to Access SAP Business ByDesign

To begin your journey with SAP Business ByDesign, you need to access the system. Follow these steps to get started:

Step 1: Open your preferred web browser.

Step 2: Enter the URL provided by your SAP Business ByDesign administrator or access the SAP Business ByDesign login page directly.

Step 3: On the login page, enter your username and password. These credentials would have been provided to you by your administrator. If you are logging in for the first time, make sure to change your password as per the system's password policy.

Step 4: Select the appropriate system from the dropdown menu if you have access to multiple systems. This step is usually relevant for administrators or users working in different company divisions.

Step 5: Click on the "Log On" button to access SAP Business ByDesign.

1.5 Navigating the User Interface

Once you have logged in successfully, you will be greeted by the SAP Business ByDesign user interface. Let's take a quick tour of the main elements to familiarize yourself with the interface:

a. Home Screen: The home screen is your starting point after logging in. It provides an overview of your work center view and displays key information and widgets specific to your role.

b. Work Center: The work center is where you will spend most of your time performing tasks related to your job role. It consists of various work center views, such as the Overview, Sales, Purchasing, Projects, and more. Each work center view provides access to specific modules and functionalities.

c. Navigation Bar: The navigation bar is located at the top of the screen and contains menus and links to different areas of the system. It allows you to switch between work center views, access your favorites, search for specific transactions or reports, and access system settings.

d. Quick Create: The quick create bar is a convenient feature that allows you to create new documents or records directly from any screen. It provides shortcuts to commonly used transactions, making it easier to initiate new processes.

e. Subscreens and Work Areas: Within each work center view, you will find various subscreens and work areas. These areas contain specific information, records, or functionalities related to the selected module. For example, in the Sales work center, you may have subscreens for Leads, Opportunities, Quotations, and Sales Orders.

f. Data Fields and Buttons: Throughout the user interface, you will encounter data fields, dropdown menus, checkboxes, and buttons. These elements allow you to enter or select data, perform actions, and navigate through the system.

1.6 Customizing Your Workspace

SAP Business ByDesign offers flexibility in customizing your workspace to suit your preferences and work requirements. Here are some customization options you can explore:

a. Personalizing the Work Center: You can personalize your work center view by adding or removing work center views, rearranging them, or creating your own custom views. This allows you to tailor the interface to display the modules and functionalities you frequently use.

b. Favorites and Shortcuts: You can mark specific transactions, reports, or screens as favorites to access them quickly. Additionally, you can create shortcuts to specific areas or functions within the system, saving you time and effort.

c. Adapting Table Layouts: When viewing tables or lists of data, you can adjust the columns displayed, change the order of columns, and apply filters or sorting options. This customization helps you focus on relevant information and simplifies data analysis.

d. Role-Based Adaptations: Depending on your role or job function, you may have access to different functionalities or fields within the system. Administrators can configure role-based adaptations to ensure users have the appropriate access and visibility.

Congratulations! You have completed the second section of Chapter 1, where we explored how to access SAP Business ByDesign and navigate its user interface. In the next section, we will continue with the setup process by guiding you through the initial configuration steps of your SAP Business ByDesign account.

Stay tuned for the upcoming chapter, where we delve deeper into the configuration aspects and provide you with a solid foundation to start using SAP Business ByDesign effectively!

1.7 Setting up Your SAP Business ByDesign Account

Once you have accessed SAP Business ByDesign, it's time to set up your account and configure it to align with your business needs. Follow the steps below to get started:

Step 1: Define Organizational Units

Begin by setting up the organizational structure of your company within SAP Business ByDesign. This involves creating units such as company codes, sales organizations, distribution channels, and plant locations.

Define the relationships and hierarchies between these organizational units to establish a clear structure for your business processes.

Step 2: Configure Business Partners

Business partners refer to customers, suppliers, and other entities that your business interacts with. Configure business partner master data by creating customer and supplier records.

Enter essential information such as contact details, addresses, payment terms, and credit limits to ensure accurate and efficient transactions.

Step 3: Customize Master Data

Customize the master data components in SAP Business ByDesign to reflect your specific business requirements.

This includes defining products and services, setting up pricing structures, creating product categories, and specifying attributes or characteristics of your offerings.

Step 4: Define Organizational Roles and Access Rights

Determine the roles and responsibilities within your organization and assign appropriate access rights to users in SAP Business ByDesign.

Define user roles, establish authorization profiles, and assign permissions to ensure that individuals have the necessary access and restrictions based on their job functions.

Step 5: Configure General Settings

Adjust the general settings of your SAP Business ByDesign account to align with your business preferences.

Configure settings such as default currencies, time zones, language preferences, and other system-wide parameters that impact how the solution functions for your organization.

Step 6: Set Up Document Templates and Number Ranges

Customize document templates, such as sales order forms or purchase order templates, to match your company's branding and communication standards.

Establish document number ranges to ensure consistency and avoid conflicts when generating transactional documents.

Step 7: Enable Integration with External Systems

If your organization needs to integrate SAP Business ByDesign with other external systems, such as customer relationship management (CRM) platforms or e-commerce solutions, configure the necessary integration settings.

Set up integration interfaces, define data exchange formats, and establish secure connections between SAP Business ByDesign and external systems.

By completing these initial setup steps, you will have a solid foundation for using SAP Business ByDesign effectively within your organization. In the next chapter, we will explore the various modules and functionalities of SAP Business ByDesign in greater detail.

Congratulations! You have now completed the section on setting up your SAP Business ByDesign account. In the upcoming chapters, we will dive deeper into each module, guiding you through the key functionalities and best practices for using SAP Business ByDesign to streamline your business processes.

Stay tuned for an exciting journey ahead, where you'll acquire the knowledge and skills to master SAP Business ByDesign!

Chapter 2: Managing Master Data

In this chapter, we will explore the essential task of managing master data in SAP Business ByDesign. Master data refers to the core information that underlies your business processes, such as customer data, product information, and organizational units. Proper management of master data is crucial for the smooth operation of your business. Let's dive in!

2.1 Creating and Maintaining Organizational Units

Organizational units represent the structure of your company within SAP Business ByDesign. They define various entities such as company codes, sales organizations, distribution channels, and plant locations. Follow these steps to create and maintain organizational units:

Step 1: Access the Organizational Management work center view.

Step 2: Create Organizational Units:

Select the relevant organizational unit type (e.g., Company, Sales Organization) and click on the "New" button.

Provide the required details, such as the name, description, and any additional information specific to the unit type.

Save the changes.

Step 3: Define Relationships and Hierarchies:

Establish relationships between different organizational units to reflect the structure and reporting lines within your organization.

Assign parent and child units to create a hierarchical structure.

Specify the relationships, such as sales organizations linked to specific distribution channels.

Step 4: Maintain Organizational Data:

Regularly update organizational data as your company evolves.

Make necessary changes to reflect organizational restructurings, new divisions, or any modifications required to align with your business operations.

2.2 Configuring Business Partners

Business partners are entities that your business interacts with, including customers, suppliers, and prospects. Configuring business partner data is vital for effective sales, purchasing, and customer relationship management. Follow these steps to configure business partners:

Step 1: Access the Business Partners work center view.

Step 2: Create Business Partner Records:

Select the appropriate business partner category (Customer, Supplier) and click on the "New" button.

Enter relevant information, such as contact details, addresses, payment terms, and credit limits.

Save the changes.

Step 3: Maintain Business Partner Data:

Regularly update business partner data to ensure accuracy and reflect any changes in contact information or business relationships.

Monitor credit limits and payment terms to manage credit risk and establish smooth transactional processes.

Step 4: Establish Business Partner Relationships:

Establish relationships between business partners to reflect affiliations, parent-child connections, or partner hierarchies.

This is particularly useful for managing complex customer relationships or supplier networks.

2.3 Managing Products and Services

Proper management of product and service information is essential for sales, procurement, and inventory management processes. Follow these steps to manage products and services in SAP Business ByDesign:

Step 1: Access the Product and Service Management work center view.

Step 2: Create Product and Service Records:

Select the appropriate product category (e.g., Finished Goods, Raw Materials) and click on the "New" button.

Enter essential information, such as product descriptions, pricing details, units of measure, and any other relevant attributes.

Save the changes.

Step 3: Maintain Product and Service Data:

Regularly update product and service data to reflect changes in pricing, specifications, or any other pertinent information.

Monitor stock levels, reorder points, and lead times to ensure efficient inventory management.

Step 4: Categorize and Classify Products:

Assign product categories and classifications to facilitate easy identification and grouping of products.

This helps streamline sales processes, enables effective reporting, and supports targeted marketing campaigns.

Congratulations! You have completed the section on managing master data in SAP Business ByDesign. In the next chapter, we will explore the Sales and Marketing module, where we will guide you through the process of creating sales orders, managing customer relationships, and tracking marketing campaigns.

Stay tuned for an exciting journey ahead, where you'll gain the knowledge and skills to effectively utilize SAP Business ByDesign's Sales and Marketing capabilities!

Chapter 3: Sales and Marketing

In this chapter, we will dive into the Sales and Marketing module of SAP Business ByDesign. This module empowers you to efficiently manage your sales processes, build strong customer relationships, and drive effective marketing campaigns. Let's explore the key functionalities and learn how to leverage them effectively.

3.1 Creating Sales Orders and Quotations

Sales orders and quotations are essential documents for managing your sales processes. SAP Business ByDesign offers robust features to create and manage these documents. Follow these steps to create sales orders and quotations:

Step 1: Access the Sales Orders or Quotations work center view.

Step 2: Create a New Sales Order or Quotation:

Click on the "New" button to create a new sales order or quotation.

Enter relevant information such as customer details, products/services, quantities, pricing, and delivery information.

Save the document.

Step 3: Review and Confirm Sales Orders or Quotations:

Before finalizing a sales order or quotation, review the details for accuracy.

Confirm the document to proceed with further processing.

Step 4: Manage Sales Order Fulfillment:

Once a sales order is confirmed, manage the order fulfillment process.

Monitor order status, track deliveries, and manage stock allocation to ensure timely order processing.

Step 5: Create Deliveries and Invoices:

Generate deliveries based on confirmed sales orders to prepare for shipment.

Create invoices based on delivered goods or services to bill customers accurately.

3.2 Managing Customer Relationships

Building strong customer relationships is crucial for business success. SAP Business ByDesign provides tools to manage customer data, track interactions, and enhance customer engagement. Follow these steps to manage customer relationships effectively:

Step 1: Access the Customers work center view.

Step 2: Maintain Customer Data:

Create and update customer records with accurate and up-to-date information.

Include details such as contact information, addresses, communication preferences, and customer classifications.

Step 3: Track Interactions:

Record customer interactions such as phone calls, emails, and meetings.

Log activities and follow-ups to ensure effective communication and timely response.

Step 4: Monitor Sales Opportunities:

Track and manage sales opportunities associated with each customer.

Update opportunity stages, probability, and expected revenue to monitor the progress of potential deals.

Step 5: Analyze Customer Data:

Utilize reporting and analytics features to gain insights into customer behavior and preferences.

Identify trends, assess sales performance, and make data-driven decisions to improve customer satisfaction.

3.3 Tracking Marketing Campaigns

Marketing campaigns play a vital role in reaching and engaging your target audience. SAP Business ByDesign enables you to plan, execute, and track your marketing efforts efficiently. Follow these steps to track marketing campaigns:

Step 1: Access the Marketing work center view.

Step 2: Plan Marketing Campaigns:

Create marketing campaigns with clear objectives, target audience, and desired outcomes.

Define campaign budgets, timelines, and marketing channels to be used.

Step 3: Execute Marketing Activities:

Implement marketing activities such as email campaigns, social media promotions, and events.

Monitor campaign progress and ensure activities are executed according to plan.

Step 4: Track Campaign Response:

Capture and track campaign responses to evaluate their effectiveness.

Analyze response rates, lead conversions, and campaign ROI to assess the success of your marketing initiatives.

Step 5: Analyze Marketing Performance:

Utilize reporting and analytics features to analyze marketing performance.

Measure key metrics, identify successful campaigns, and optimize future marketing strategies.

Congratulations! You have completed the section on the Sales and Marketing module in SAP Business ByDesign. In the next chapter, we will explore the Procurement and Inventory Management module, where we will guide you through the procurement process, vendor management, and inventory control.

Get ready for an exciting journey ahead as we uncover the functionalities and best practices of SAP Business ByDesign!

Chapter 4: Procurement and Inventory Management

In this chapter, we will delve into the Procurement and Inventory Management module of SAP Business ByDesign. This module allows you to streamline your procurement processes, manage vendor relationships, and optimize inventory control. Let's explore the key functionalities and learn how to leverage them effectively.

4.1 Purchase Requisitions and Orders

The procurement process starts with creating purchase requisitions and subsequently generating purchase orders to request and acquire goods or services. Follow these steps to create purchase requisitions and orders in SAP Business ByDesign:

Step 1: Access the Purchase Requisitions or Purchase Orders work center view.

Step 2: Create a New Purchase Requisition:

Click on the "New" button to create a new purchase requisition.

Enter the details such as material or service requirements, quantities, delivery dates, and other relevant information.

Save the purchase requisition.

Step 3: Review and Approve Purchase Requisitions:

Review the details of the purchase requisition for accuracy and completeness.

Submit the purchase requisition for approval according to your organization's procurement approval process.

Step 4: Convert Purchase Requisitions into Purchase Orders:

Once the purchase requisition is approved, convert it into a purchase order.

Verify the information, make any necessary adjustments, and confirm the purchase order.

Step 5: Manage Purchase Order Processing:

Monitor the status of purchase orders, track deliveries, and manage the procurement process.

Communicate with vendors, track order confirmations, and ensure timely delivery of goods or services.

4.2 Vendor Management

Effective vendor management is crucial for successful procurement. SAP Business ByDesign provides tools to manage vendor data, track vendor performance, and streamline communication. Follow these steps to manage vendor relationships:

Step 1: Access the Suppliers work center view.

Step 2: Maintain Vendor Data:

Create and update vendor records with accurate and up-to-date information.

Include details such as contact information, addresses, payment terms, and vendor classifications.

Step 3: Track Vendor Performance:

Monitor vendor performance based on factors such as delivery reliability, quality of goods or services, and adherence to agreed-upon terms.

Analyze vendor performance metrics to identify areas of improvement and make informed decisions regarding vendor selection.

Step 4: Manage Contracts and Agreements:

Maintain contracts and agreements with vendors, including terms and conditions, pricing agreements, and service-level agreements.

Monitor contract expiration dates and initiate renewals or renegotiations as necessary.

Step 5: Communicate with Vendors:

Utilize communication tools within SAP Business ByDesign to collaborate effectively with vendors.

Exchange messages, share documents, and maintain a clear line of communication for smooth procurement processes.

4.3 Inventory Control and Optimization

Efficient inventory management is crucial for minimizing costs and ensuring product availability. SAP Business ByDesign provides features to track and optimize inventory levels. Follow these steps to manage inventory effectively:

Step 1: Access the Materials and Inventory work center view.

Step 2: Maintain Material Master Data:

Create and update material master records with accurate and detailed information.

Include details such as material descriptions, units of measure, pricing, and stock-keeping information.

Step 3: Monitor Stock Levels:

Track inventory levels for each material to ensure adequate stock availability.

Set up alerts and notifications for low-stock situations to trigger replenishment processes.

Step 4: Optimize Replenishment:

Utilize reorder point planning or materials requirements planning (MRP) functionality to automate and optimize the replenishment process.

Set up reorder points, safety stock levels, and lead times to ensure timely replenishment of inventory.

Step 5: Perform Physical Inventory:

Conduct regular physical inventory checks to reconcile system records with actual stock on hand.

Perform stock counts, update inventory records, and address any discrepancies or issues identified.

Congratulations! You have completed the section on the Procurement and Inventory Management module in SAP Business ByDesign. In the next chapter, we will explore the Financial Management module, where we will guide you through the key functionalities of general ledger accounting, accounts payable and receivable, and cash management.

Get ready to enhance your financial management processes with SAP Business ByDesign!

Chapter 5: Financial Management

In this chapter, we will dive into the Financial Management module of SAP Business ByDesign. This module enables you to effectively manage your company's financial processes, including general ledger accounting, accounts payable and receivable, and cash management. Let's explore the key functionalities and learn how to leverage them effectively.

5.1 General Ledger Accounting

General Ledger Accounting is the foundation of your financial management processes. It allows you to record, track, and analyze your company's financial transactions. Follow these steps to utilize the General Ledger Accounting functionality in SAP Business ByDesign:

Step 1: Access the General Ledger work center view.

Step 2: Define Chart of Accounts:

Set up your company's chart of accounts, which defines the structure and organization of your financial accounts.

Configure account groups, account hierarchies, and assign relevant attributes to each account.

Step 3: Create and Post Journal Entries:

Create journal entries to record financial transactions such as revenue, expenses, assets, liabilities, and equity changes.

Enter the appropriate accounts, amounts, and any additional details required for each entry.

Post the journal entries to update the general ledger.

Step 4: Perform Account Reconciliations:

Reconcile your general ledger accounts with supporting documents or statements.

Match transactions, verify balances, and resolve any discrepancies to ensure accurate financial reporting.

Step 5: Generate Financial Reports:

Utilize the reporting and analytics capabilities of SAP Business ByDesign to generate financial reports.

Analyze your company's financial performance, review balance sheets, income statements, and cash flow statements to gain insights into your financial health.

5.2 Accounts Payable and Receivable

Efficient management of accounts payable and receivable is crucial for maintaining healthy cash flow and strong vendor/customer relationships. Follow these steps to effectively manage accounts payable and receivable in SAP Business ByDesign:

Step 1: Access the Accounts Payable or Accounts Receivable work center view.

Step 2: Manage Vendor Invoices (Accounts Payable):

Receive and process vendor invoices, ensuring accuracy and compliance.

Verify invoice details, match them with purchase orders or goods receipts, and validate against agreed-upon terms.

Create and post vendor invoices to update accounts payable.

Step 3: Monitor and Manage Payments (Accounts Payable):

Track due dates and payment terms for outstanding vendor invoices.

Initiate payment processes, including payment runs and disbursements, based on approved payment methods.

Manage vendor payment reconciliations and maintain a clear record of payment transactions.

Step 4: Manage Customer Invoices (Accounts Receivable):

Create and send customer invoices, ensuring accuracy and compliance.

Include relevant details such as billing items, pricing, terms, and any additional charges or discounts.

Post customer invoices to update accounts receivable.

Step 5: Monitor and Collect Receivables (Accounts Receivable):

Monitor customer account balances, aging, and payment status.

Manage customer collections processes, including reminders, dunning letters, and escalation procedures.

Record and reconcile customer payments to update accounts receivable and ensure accurate financial records.

5.3 Cash Management and Bank Reconciliation

Efficient cash management and bank reconciliation processes help you maintain visibility into your company's cash flow and ensure accurate financial reporting. Follow these steps to manage cash and perform bank reconciliations in SAP Business ByDesign:

Step 1: Access the Cash and Liquidity Management work center view.

Step 2: Manage Bank Accounts:

Set up and maintain your company's bank accounts in SAP Business ByDesign.

Include relevant details such as account numbers, bank information, and currency specifications.

Step 3: Record Cash Transactions:

Record incoming and outgoing cash transactions such as payments, receipts, and transfers.

Associate transactions with the appropriate bank accounts and relevant general ledger accounts.

Step 4: Perform Bank Reconciliations:

Reconcile your bank statements with your recorded cash transactions.

Match transactions, verify balances, and identify any discrepancies or outstanding items.

Perform regular bank reconciliations to ensure accurate cash reporting.

Step 5: Monitor Cash Flow and Forecasting:

Utilize cash flow forecasting tools within SAP Business ByDesign to monitor and predict your company's cash position.

Analyze cash flow trends, forecast future cash requirements, and make informed financial decisions.

Congratulations! You have completed the section on the Financial Management module in SAP Business ByDesign. In the next chapter, we will explore the Project Management module, where we will guide you through the key functionalities of setting up and managing projects, resource allocation, and project progress monitoring.

Get ready to optimize your project management processes with SAP Business ByDesign!

Chapter 6: Project Management

In this chapter, we will explore the Project Management module of SAP Business ByDesign. This module enables you to effectively plan, execute, and monitor projects within your organization. Whether you are handling internal projects or providing services to clients, SAP Business ByDesign offers robust functionalities to streamline your project management processes. Let's explore the key features and learn how to leverage them effectively.

6.1 Setting Up and Managing Projects

Effective project management begins with proper project setup and configuration. Follow these steps to set up and manage projects in SAP Business ByDesign:

Step 1: Access the Projects work center view.

Step 2: Create a New Project:

Click on the "New" button to create a new project.

Define the project name, description, start and end dates, project type, and other relevant information.

Save the project.

Step 3: Define Project Structure:

Create work breakdown structures (WBS) to break down the project into manageable tasks and sub-tasks.

Assign resources, set milestones, and establish dependencies between tasks.

Define project phases, activities, and deliverables to ensure clarity and structure.

Step 4: Plan Project Budget:

Define the project budget by allocating costs to different project elements.

Assign costs to resources, materials, and other project-related expenses.

Monitor and track project costs against the allocated budget throughout the project lifecycle.

Step 5: Assign Project Team Members:

Assign project team members to their respective roles and responsibilities.

Define resource availability, capacity, and allocation to ensure efficient resource management.

6.2 Resource Allocation and Planning

Effective resource allocation is vital for project success. SAP Business ByDesign provides features to allocate resources efficiently and ensure optimal utilization. Follow these steps to manage resource allocation in SAP Business ByDesign:

Step 1: Access the Resource Management work center view.

Step 2: Define Resource Pool:

Create a resource pool consisting of available resources within your organization.

Include employees, contractors, equipment, and other relevant resources.

Define resource skills, availability, and utilization rates.

Step 3: Allocate Resources to Projects:

Assign resources to project tasks based on their availability, skills, and workload.

Utilize resource availability and utilization views to identify the best-fit resources for each task.

Optimize resource allocation to balance workloads and ensure timely project delivery.

Step 4: Monitor Resource Utilization:

Track resource utilization to identify potential bottlenecks or resource constraints.

Analyze resource capacity and availability to make informed decisions regarding resource allocation.

6.3 Monitoring and Controlling Project Progress

Monitoring and controlling project progress is crucial to ensure projects stay on track and meet their objectives. SAP Business ByDesign offers tools to monitor and control project activities effectively. Follow these steps to monitor and control project progress:

Step 1: Access the Project Control work center view.

Step 2: Track Project Activities:

Monitor project activities, tasks, and milestones to assess progress.

Update task statuses, record actual effort, and document completion percentages.

Step 3: Manage Project Issues and Risks:

Identify and document project issues, risks, and dependencies.

Mitigate risks and resolve issues promptly to minimize project disruptions.

Step 4: Analyze Project Performance:

Utilize reporting and analytics capabilities to analyze project performance.

Generate project status reports, track key performance indicators (KPIs), and assess project health.

Step 5: Adjust Project Plans:

Modify project plans as needed based on actual progress and changing project requirements.

Update timelines, resource allocations, and budgets to reflect changes in project scope or priorities.

Congratulations! You have completed the section on the Project Management module in SAP Business ByDesign. In the next chapter, we will explore the Human Resources module, where we will guide you through the key functionalities of employee administration, time and attendance management, and performance management.

Get ready to optimize your human resources processes with SAP Business ByDesign!

Chapter 7: Human Resources

In this chapter, we will explore the Human Resources (HR) module of SAP Business ByDesign. This module provides robust features to streamline your HR processes, including employee administration, time and attendance management, and performance management. Let's dive into the key functionalities and learn how to leverage them effectively.

7.1 Employee Administration

Employee administration involves managing employee records, organizational structures, and personnel data. SAP Business ByDesign offers tools to streamline employee administration processes. Follow these steps to manage employee administration in SAP Business ByDesign:

Step 1: Access the Employee Administration work center view.

Step 2: Maintain Employee Records:

Create and update employee records with accurate and up-to-date information.

Include personal details, contact information, employment history, and other relevant data.

Step 3: Define Organizational Structures:

Configure organizational units, such as departments, teams, or cost centers.

Establish relationships and hierarchies within the organizational structure.

Step 4: Manage Employment Information:

Maintain employment-related data, such as position details, job descriptions, and contract information.

Record employee assignments, transfers, promotions, and terminations.

7.2 Time and Attendance Management

Efficient time and attendance management is essential for accurate payroll processing and workforce productivity tracking. SAP Business ByDesign provides features to manage time and attendance effectively. Follow these steps to manage time and attendance in SAP Business ByDesign:

Step 1: Access the Time and Attendance work center view.

Step 2: Define Time Recording Profiles:

Configure time recording profiles based on your organization's time management policies.

Define work schedules, break rules, overtime rules, and absence types.

Step 3: Record Employee Time Data:

Record employee attendance, absences, and time entries.

Utilize timesheet functionality or time recording devices for accurate time tracking.

Step 4: Manage Time Approvals and Workflows:

Set up approval workflows to ensure proper review and validation of recorded time data.

Define approval hierarchies, time period validations, and approval rules.

7.3 Performance Management

Effective performance management allows you to align employee goals with organizational objectives, provide feedback, and assess performance. SAP Business ByDesign offers features to manage performance effectively. Follow these steps to manage performance in SAP Business ByDesign:

Step 1: Access the Performance Management work center view.

Step 2: Define Performance Appraisal Templates:

Configure performance appraisal templates based on your organization's performance management process.

Define appraisal criteria, goal setting sections, competency assessments, and feedback mechanisms.

Step 3: Set Employee Goals:

Create and track employee goals aligned with organizational objectives.

Set SMART (Specific, Measurable, Achievable, Relevant, Time-bound) goals to ensure clarity and accountability.

Step 4: Conduct Performance Appraisals:

Initiate and conduct performance appraisal cycles based on defined timelines.

Utilize the appraisal templates to assess employee performance, provide feedback, and identify development areas.

Step 5: Performance Analytics and Development:

Utilize reporting and analytics capabilities to analyze performance data and identify trends.

Use performance insights to guide talent development initiatives, training programs, and succession planning.

Congratulations! You have completed the section on the Human Resources module in SAP Business ByDesign. In the next chapter, we will explore the Reporting and Analytics capabilities, where we will guide you through creating custom reports and dashboards, analyzing data, and gaining real-time insights for decision making.

Get ready to unlock the power of data with SAP Business ByDesign!

Chapter 8: Reporting and Analytics

In this chapter, we will explore the Reporting and Analytics capabilities of SAP Business ByDesign. These features enable you to gather insights from your data, create custom reports and dashboards, and make informed decisions for your organization. Let's dive into the key functionalities and learn how to leverage them effectively.

8.1 Data Analysis and Reporting

SAP Business ByDesign provides robust tools to analyze your data and generate insightful reports. Follow these steps to perform data analysis and reporting:

Step 1: Access the Analytics work center view.

Step 2: Select a Data Source:

Choose the relevant data source from the available options, such as sales, procurement, finance, or project data.

Specify the data attributes and filters to refine your data selection.

Step 3: Create Custom Reports:

Utilize the report designer tool to create custom reports tailored to your specific requirements.

Define report layouts, select data fields, apply filters, and choose visualization options.

Step 4: Save and Share Reports:

Save your custom reports for future use and easy access.

Share reports with relevant stakeholders within your organization.

8.2 Dashboards and Key Performance Indicators (KPIs)

Dashboards and KPIs provide a visual representation of your organization's key metrics and performance indicators. Follow these steps to create and utilize dashboards and KPIs:

Step 1: Access the Dashboards work center view.

Step 2: Create Custom Dashboards:

Use the dashboard designer tool to create personalized dashboards that display relevant data and KPIs.

Select widgets, define data sources, and configure visualization options.

Step 3: Monitor Key Metrics:

Populate your dashboards with KPIs that reflect the performance of your organization.

Monitor key metrics such as revenue, expenses, customer satisfaction, or project progress.

Step 4: Analyze Trends and Drill-Down:

Utilize interactive features to analyze trends, drill down into specific data subsets, and identify areas for improvement.

Gain deeper insights into your organization's performance and make data-driven decisions.

8.3 Real-Time Data Insights

SAP Business ByDesign provides real-time data insights, enabling you to make informed decisions based on up-to-date information. Follow these steps to leverage real-time data insights:

Step 1: Access the Analytics work center view.

Step 2: Utilize Interactive Data Exploration:

Leverage interactive features to explore your data in real-time.

Apply filters, drill down into specific data points, and analyze data subsets on the fly.

Step 3: Utilize Predictive Analytics:

Leverage predictive analytics capabilities to identify patterns, trends, and potential future outcomes.

Utilize predictive models to make informed predictions and optimize your decision-making processes.

Step 4: Monitor Performance and Alerts:

Set up alerts and notifications to monitor key performance indicators and receive notifications when specific thresholds are reached.

Stay informed about critical changes in your organization's performance.

Congratulations! You have completed the section on Reporting and Analytics in SAP Business ByDesign. In the next chapter, we will explore the Integration and Collaboration capabilities, where we will guide you through integrating SAP Business ByDesign with other systems and leveraging collaborative features to enhance communication and productivity.

Get ready to connect and collaborate with SAP Business ByDesign!

Chapter 9: Integration and Collaboration

In this chapter, we will explore the Integration and Collaboration capabilities of SAP Business ByDesign. These features enable you to integrate your SAP Business ByDesign system with other systems and collaborate effectively within your organization. Let's dive into the key functionalities and learn how to leverage them effectively.

9.1 System Integration

Integrating SAP Business ByDesign with other systems allows for seamless data exchange and process automation. Follow these steps to integrate SAP Business ByDesign with external systems:

Step 1: Identify Integration Requirements:

Determine the systems you need to integrate with SAP Business ByDesign, such as CRM, e-commerce platforms, or third-party applications.

Define the scope and objectives of the integration project.

Step 2: Configure Integration Scenarios:

Utilize the Integration and Communication Management work center view to configure integration scenarios.

Define integration interfaces, data exchange formats, and authentication methods.

Step 3: Set Up Data Mapping and Transformation:

Map the data fields and structures between SAP Business ByDesign and the external system.

Define data transformation rules to ensure compatibility and consistency.

Step 4: Test and Validate Integration:

Perform testing and validation to ensure seamless data exchange between systems.

Verify data accuracy, system responses, and error handling.

9.2 Collaboration and Communication

Collaboration and communication tools within SAP Business ByDesign facilitate effective teamwork and streamline internal communication processes. Follow these steps to leverage collaboration and communication features:

Step 1: Access the Collaboration work center view.

Step 2: Utilize Business Communication Tools:

Utilize features such as email integration, discussion forums, and chat functionality to foster collaboration.

Communicate with team members, share documents, and track discussions within the system.

Step 3: Set Up Workflow and Approvals:

Configure workflow processes for approvals, notifications, and document routing.

Define approval chains, notification triggers, and escalation procedures.

Step 4: Enable Document Sharing and Collaboration:

Utilize document management features to store and share documents within your organization.

Collaborate on documents, track revisions, and maintain version control.

9.3 Mobile and Remote Access

SAP Business ByDesign offers mobile and remote access capabilities, allowing you to access the system on the go and from remote locations. Follow these steps to leverage mobile and remote access:

Step 1: Install the Mobile App:

Download and install the SAP Business ByDesign mobile app on your mobile device.

Authenticate using your SAP Business ByDesign credentials.

Step 2: Access SAP Business ByDesign Remotely:

Utilize secure remote access methods, such as virtual private networks (VPNs), to access SAP Business ByDesign from remote locations.

Ensure adherence to your organization's security policies.

Step 3: Perform Key Tasks and Activities:

Access relevant work center views, perform key tasks, and view important data using the mobile app or remote access.

Stay connected and productive even when away from the office.

Congratulations! You have completed the section on Integration and Collaboration in SAP Business ByDesign. In the next chapter, we will explore the Administration and System Configuration aspects, where we will guide you through system administration tasks, user management, and system configuration settings.

Get ready to become an SAP Business ByDesign administrator and configure your system for optimal performance!

Chapter 10: Administration and System Configuration

In this final chapter, we will explore the Administration and System Configuration aspects of SAP Business ByDesign. As an administrator, you will be responsible for managing system settings, user accounts, and maintaining the overall performance of your SAP Business ByDesign instance. Let's dive into the key functionalities and learn how to leverage them effectively.

10.1 System Administration

System administration involves managing and maintaining your SAP Business ByDesign instance. Follow these steps to perform system administration tasks:

Step 1: Access the Administrator work center view.

Step 2: Manage System Configuration:

Configure system-wide settings such as default currencies, time zones, language preferences, and other parameters.

Customize the user interface, themes, and branding elements to align with your organization's identity.

Step 3: Monitor System Performance:

Monitor system performance and resource utilization to ensure optimal system operation.

Identify and address any performance bottlenecks or issues that may impact user experience.

Step 4: Perform System Backups and Restorations:

Establish regular backup schedules to safeguard your data.

Perform system backups and test restoration procedures to ensure data recoverability.

10.2 User and Access Management

Managing user accounts and access rights is essential for maintaining system security and controlling user permissions. Follow these steps to manage user accounts and access rights:

Step 1: Access the User and Access Management work center view.

Step 2: Create User Accounts:

Create user accounts for individuals who will access SAP Business ByDesign.

Define user roles and assign appropriate access rights based on job functions.

Step 3: Manage User Permissions:

Set up authorization profiles and assign them to user roles.

Define granular access rights to specific work center views, reports, and system functionalities.

Step 4: Perform User Administration:

Maintain user accounts by updating personal information, passwords, and user preferences.

Manage user access requests, approvals, and terminations as needed.

10.3 System Configuration

System configuration involves tailoring SAP Business ByDesign to meet your organization's specific requirements. Follow these steps to perform system configuration:

Step 1: Access the Business Configuration work center view.

Step 2: Configure Business Scenarios:

Define business scenarios relevant to your organization, such as sales, procurement, finance, or project management.

Customize configuration settings to align with your specific business processes and requirements.

Step 3: Adapt Business Processes:

Customize standard business processes to meet your organization's specific needs.

Define workflows, approval processes, document templates, and other process-related settings.

Step 4: Maintain Master Data Configuration:

Update and maintain master data configuration settings.

Customize product categories, pricing structures, organizational units, and other master data components.

Congratulations! You have completed the section on Administration and System Configuration in SAP Business ByDesign. With these skills, you are equipped to manage and configure your SAP Business ByDesign instance effectively.

Thank you for joining us on this learning journey. We hope this tutorial book has provided you with valuable insights and knowledge to leverage SAP Business ByDesign for your organization's success. Remember to stay updated with the latest features and enhancements to make the most of this powerful business management solution.

Best wishes for your SAP Business ByDesign endeavors!

Conclusion

Congratulations on completing this tutorial book on Learn SAP Business ByDesign! By now, you have gained a comprehensive understanding of the key functionalities and capabilities of SAP Business ByDesign. You are equipped with the knowledge to effectively manage various aspects of your business, including master data, sales and marketing, procurement and inventory management, financial management, project management, human resources, reporting and analytics, integration and collaboration, and system administration.

As you continue your journey with SAP Business ByDesign, remember to stay curious and explore additional resources such as SAP documentation, online forums, and training materials to deepen your expertise. The world of SAP Business ByDesign is dynamic and ever-evolving, with new features and enhancements being introduced regularly.

Now it's time to put your newfound knowledge into practice. Whether you are implementing SAP Business ByDesign for your organization or seeking to enhance your existing usage, you have the tools and understanding to make the most of this robust business management solution.

Thank you for joining us on this learning adventure. We hope this tutorial book has been valuable in your quest to master

SAP Business ByDesign. Best of luck in your future endeavors, and may SAP Business ByDesign empower you to achieve your business goals.

Happy exploring and may your business thrive with SAP Business ByDesign!

www.ingramcontent.com/pod-product-compliance
Lightning Source LLC
LaVergne TN
LVHW051613050326
832903LV00033B/4476